The Busy Beavers

Story by Beverley Randell
Illustrations by Elizabeth Russell-Arnot

NELSON PRICE MILBURN

A father beaver, a mother beaver
and their four little beavers
lived in a home in a lake.

Their home was a little island
with a secret tunnel
that went down into the water.
They were safe on the island.
The bears and the foxes
and the great wild cats
could not get them.

3

The beavers had made the island
from sticks and stones and mud.

They had made a long dam, too.
The dam kept the lake
filled with water.

Lap, lap, lap,
went the water, all day long,
as the beavers slept.

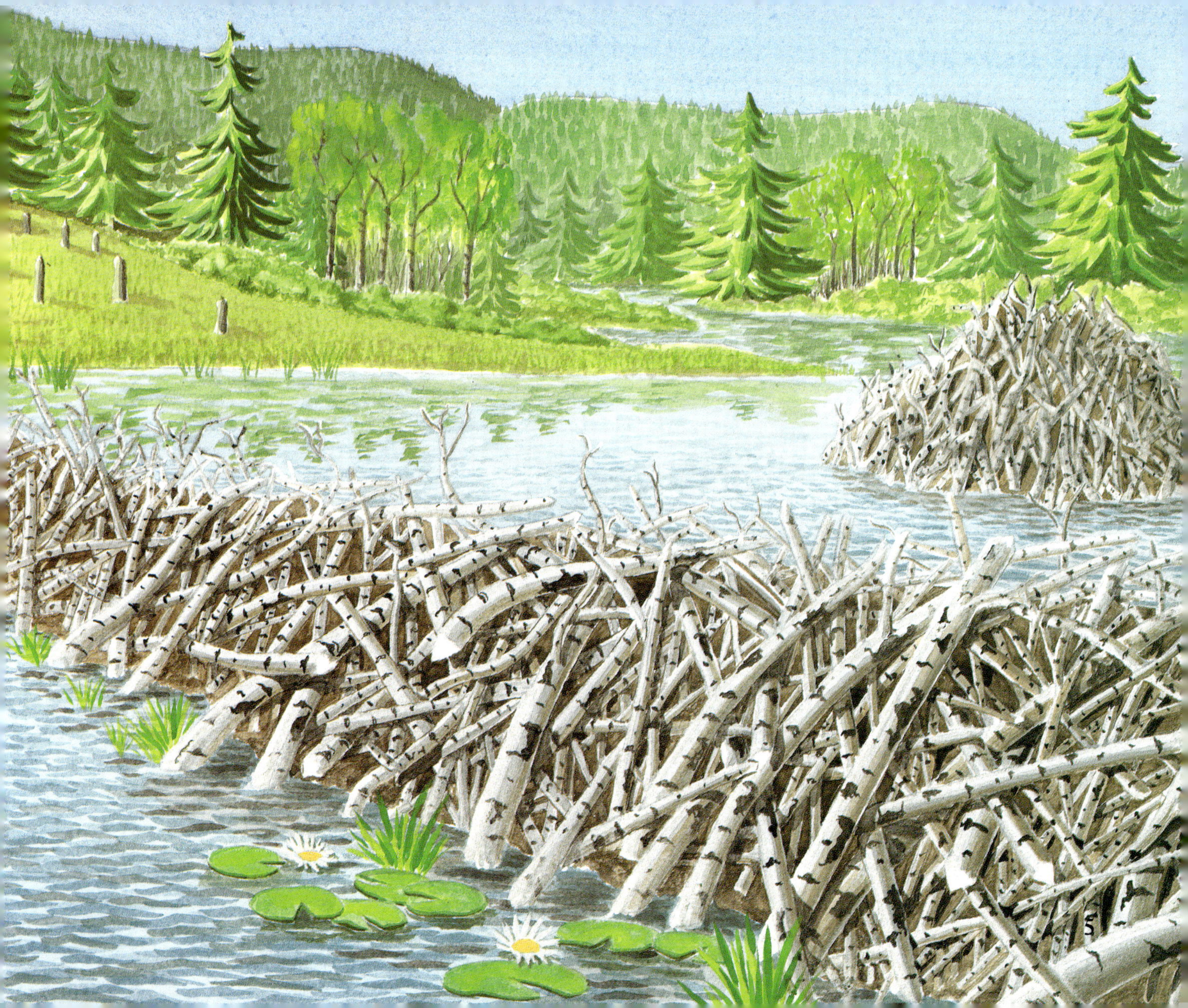

One spring evening,
the father beaver woke up.
Something was not right!
The water in the lake
was going down.

He went into the tunnel
and slipped down into the water.
He swam across the lake
to look at the dam.

7

When the father beaver got to the dam
he saw that it was broken.
Water was pouring out of a big hole.

Slap! went his tail on the water.
Slap!
All the beaver family woke up
and swam to help him.

9

They hurried off
to get sticks and mud
to put in the hole.

But the hole was too big.
Water was running out very fast.
As soon as a stick was put
into the hole,
it was washed away.

The water in the lake
went down
    and down
        and down.

11

The father beaver swam
across the lake to the forest.
He needed some bigger branches.

He went round and round a tree,
cutting into it with his teeth.
At last the tree fell down.
Crash!

The mother beaver
and the four little beavers
went to help him with the branches.

13

All the beavers swam back to the dam
with branches in their mouths.
They pushed the biggest branches
into the hole first.
Slowly the hole got smaller.

The busy beavers found more sticks
and more stones
and more mud.

They worked all night.

15

By morning the dam was fixed.
The tired beavers swam home to sleep.
The lake filled with water again.

Once more
the beavers were safe
inside their home.

Lap, lap, lap,
went the water.
Lap, lap, lap,
and the beavers slept.